Not Hearing the Wood Thrush

MARGARET GIBSON

Not Hearing the Wood Thrush

POEMS

LOUISIANA STATE UNIVERSITY PRESS

BATON ROUGE

Published by Louisiana State University Press
Copyright © 2018 by Margaret Gibson
All rights reserved
Manufactured in the United States of America
LSU Press Paperback Original

Designer: Laura Roubique Gleason
Typeface: Adobe Jenson Pro
Printer and binder: LSI

Acknowledgments

The author expresses gratitude to the editors of the following publications in which the poems listed first appeared, sometimes in slightly different forms: *Blackbird*: "Continuing the Story," "Door," "Soap," and "Story"; *Chautauqua*: "The Door" and "Not Knowing"; *Freshwater*: "Spring Raking" and "A Whisper"; *Georgia Review*: "Not Hearing the Wood Thrush" and, as a chapbook: "After Innocence," "The Full Catastrophe," "Isolable," "Motive for Praise, Perhaps," "Not to Remain Altogether Silent," "Open Window," "Praise," "Richer than Prayer or Vow," "Rude Drift," "Two Trees," and "Unconditional"; *Gettysburg Review*: "Big Wind," "Genesis," and "Ripe"; *Image*: "Evolution," "How Long the Long Winter," "Middle Distance, Morning," "Night Thoughts," and "Riverkeeper"; *Roanoke Review*: "Passage" ("And then the bird flew into my body . . ."); *Shenandoah*: "Playing Mozart at the Town Dump"; *Southern Review*: "Old Cloth," "Passage" ("Once in sunlight . . .), and "Without Thinking about It"; *Yale Review*: "Clouds and Moon."

A few of the images in "Continuing the Story" owe a debt of gratitude to imagery in David Hinton's book *Hunger Mountain: A Field Guide to Mind and Landscape.*

"Passage" ("Once in sunlight . . .) was published in *The Best Poems of 2017*, Natasha Trethewey, guest editor; David Lehman, series editor.

Library of Congress Cataloging-in-Publication Data

Names: Gibson, Margaret, 1944– author.
Title: Not hearing the wood thrush : poems / Margaret Gibson.
Description: Baton Rouge : Louisiana State University Press, [2018]
Identifiers: LCCN 2017055809 | ISBN 9780807168202 (pbk. : alk. paper) | ISBN 9780807168219 (pdf) | ISBN 9780807168226 (epub)
Classification: LCC PS3557.I1916 A6 2018 | DDC 811/.54—dc23
LC record available at https://lccn.loc.gov/2017055809

This book is dedicated to Ellen, for so many years my dearest friend.

This book is also for Marilyn, who lent me her place by the river.

And this book is for David, beloved David.

How can you hide from what never goes away?
  —Heraclitus

Let what comes, come; let what goes, go. Find out what remains.
  —Ramana Maharshi

Contents

Not Hearing the Wood Thrush

Not Hearing the Wood Thrush

There are thoughts that come to the door screen summer nights,
lured by a light kept on by
some childhood fear. They bump up against it, or cling.

Darkness frees them.

There is love comes late, in darkness, and gives no reason.
Body speckled, sweet as a pear.
How nakedly
the heart bears its weight.

At dusk, deep in the summer woods, a silence.
Something that was here, expected
to continue being here,
isn't.

I see the line in my palm etched by fate and not yet
snipped. The afterlife,
what is it
if not a further body desire turns toward?

No clear edge to the universe, now the scientists tell us.

They describe an intense
fuzziness instead. World spins into other worlds as incandescent
as what arises from cocoons
ripening on the underskin of leaves and stars.

Big Wind

Outside, a sound like God
shrugging
comes through the window glass.
A friend has won a prize
for lifetime
achievement. Another friend
is in Peru, another in the Himalayas.
Normal seems to mean
size and distance and light
expanding. Daily
I contract, as a plum
shrinks close to its pit over time,
until the pit
is nearly all there is.
I wanted *soul* or *self*
or the emptiness thereof
to be a place where light
widened out,
a clearing in the dark woods,
and about that clarity
a surrounding ripeness. Well. And, well. It seems
I am a speck,
a mote,
a grain of sand, from whose vantage all else
magnifies as night
expands, pinpricked
star by star.

Genesis

What's given is space, and sun,
and a single seed stem of grass
in the wind-stir. What's given
is quicksilver
along the rim of a leaf,
and that leaf retraced in the mind,
which loves form and identity.
Is that why I pretend it's the word
alight allows me
to see the dragonfly settle
its transparency and so oddly
hunch its neck to become now
the little perplexity I feel?
I draw a circle in the air and put
myself at the center. It takes
more courage than you'd think.
But none of this
makes a story, what's unbearable
having been, for the moment, left out.

Waking Early, the Day Unborn

That dim shape at the edge
is a coyote
come to check the remains
of the winter-killed deer.
Now it slips into the shadows,
part of what is hidden from us,
that larger part of who we are.
We have our instincts, our scripts
and habits, perhaps a few
clear moments, whose trail
may have led to this moon-rinsed
dawn. Or, not.
Last night for the first time
I slept on your side of the bed.
I haven't washed the pillowcase,
wanting to keep the scent of you here.
Inevitable, incurable, slow,
your illness takes you like snowmelt
as you, who loved to track insight
to its lair, word to its hidden
root, forget
most everything once you knew.
A child, I'm told, may be born without
sufficient folds in the brain
for a verbal intelligence
to arise. Untimely ripped, come
unprepared, or wise,
we are here, it seems, to bear the mystery.
Given portions of light and dark,
given protein, spirit, hunger, patience, time.

Snowing

Mornings are best, you wrote, *before words, before appetite.*

Your words put on a coat and scarf and stand with me outside
in the hushed world.

Snow is silence made visible.

Where hemlocks edge the dark pond, a fox . . . intent,
its wind-ruffled russets flecked with silence.

In an early journal you copied passages from Blake, from Sartre,
Meister Eckhart—

so that I may listen, so that I may hear.

Slowly the field takes on the color of now your hair, as does
the fox. The fox

does not move, yet it grows lighter and appears to float
nearly to the height of the hemlocks,

where it hovers. It snows harder. And harder still.

Spring Raking

The bone's clock does not run down
as quickly as the mind's . . .

that's what I think about, raking off the garden
in a spring

that breaks records for heat—

jonquil, iris, and the deadly monkshood
already above ground,

greening shoots beneath the leaf matter,
chestnut husks,

and a tiny skull that may have been an owl's.
A friend writes of being

"rendered to the place I am."

Let's suppose home ground is that place in which
one sees what abides.

Let's suppose what abides is light,

or an emptiness that holds us
unbeknownst.

Root is a kind of shimmer that lodges beneath
even the most humble

reach of word or bud knot, song or will.

The tines must touch down
more tenderly.

Not Knowing

Late day, sun behind mountains
going blue and slate,
he climbed the steep field
back of the house, perhaps to see
wider sky, then stumbled
as the thud of pain buckled him
and took him down, face down,
in the field his parents' ashes
had sweetened. No one knew
where he was for hours—
and so starlight enters the poem,
possibly frost, and the
snort of a startled deer
happening upon him, as the men
would toward morning, looking for
him as we look now for a reason.
Had he completed his work here?
By any measure, his leaving us
seems too soon. Was he complete?
He'd completed the restoration
of his house and fields,
told his distant son he loved him,
gathered family together,
cooked the feast and carved,
passed along the gold watch
that had come to him over generations . . .
Perhaps he was ready, perhaps not.
I think something in us knows
what we do not, and I hold
that not knowing close—
it sharpens the moment, it opens
the heart.
              Years from now, or months—
too soon—I may remember him
as one would look out a window
closed against the wind and hear
the sharp call of wild geese

muffled by glass and indoor chatter.
Right now, I still hear his voice,
I still smell the cold air on his coat
when he came back into the house
full of family and laughter,
carrying an armful of wood for the fire.

Passage

Alone in the dark, I sense a door.
It is open. Beyond the door, also dark.
Before I can petition . . .
(Show me where I begin or end)
Before I can leap into metaphor . . .
(The dark is a mask, the dark is a husk
that will fall from my face,
feather by feather)
Before I can court or invite,
stall or refrain,
somewhere in the dark a wheel
turns, I breathe, and—
is it our old house? Whose furniture I know,
whose banister, whose rugs and chairs
and the light switch at the edge of
pitch and plummet?
I can smell October apples
in a bowl, rosemary
bound by black thread
and hung to dry from the rafters.
(We were happy then—or were we?)
Alone in the dark, a door. It is open.
Beyond the door, also dark . . .
(*Don't do anything,* I hear. *Just stand there.*)

Story

Tell me a story, you say, once we settle,
ready for words. *Tell me a story
about freedom.* We shift apart,
embrace, shift again. And I wonder,
aren't stories what we tell ourselves
when we are not free? It may be
that thirst and the quest to relieve
that thirst is what passes for being free.
It may be that only love is free,
arising as it wills. Do we know
what sorts and separates and seals us
apart, self-enclosed? If I could, I'd be
a river—a river carries sky on its skin.
Tell a story, you whisper. And, *Who am I,*
I muse, meaning who am I *inside* the story?
In stories as in dreams one can play
all the parts. Husk off your name,
Beloved—that's when the singing starts.
And now it starts. I begin to see a river
coursing through a meadow. I see
olive trees and the dark mouth of the cave.
I'm listening to the river and to the
singing head afloat in the river's current.

And yes, it's the severed head of Orpheus
singing, his dark hair spread out
as if on a pillow, river the only bed
that floats what's left of him
into time and space, singing. The maenads
have killed him, and he's singing,
he whose pain caused him to lose
the woman he wanted returned to life.
Is this consequence or punishment
or whim? With her, he'd been *alone*—
alone as a tree is, or a flower in the field,
a pebble, a fawn, a cloud . . . each thing
integral and entire. It had been his gift
to sing each thing forth,
his voice the god's flute. He had known
only fullness. And when Eurydice
was taken, he grieved, he went
willingly into the dark of the earth,
he bargained, he sang her back—song
now the bargain we make with loss,
and it isn't free. The price
is uncertainty. He wasn't to look back
to see if she followed. You know the story.
He couldn't bear the pain of not knowing.
So he did, he turned his head,
and he looked into the emptiness . . .

Was she there? She was, or she had been.
Trusting the gradual return of her nature
from mist to flesh, she had followed.
Her hands unfurling, the life line
in her palm once again rivering in.
Her nipples hardening in the cold dank air,
the whorls of her ear petals blooming.
She could open her eyes—but the gods
had withheld her voice. Pure transience
has no voice. She couldn't breathe
a syllable or a sigh that would let him know
she followed, approaching the light,
brighter now that she could see the river.
Blown back the moment he looked into her eyes.
Dissolving back into a mist. You know how mist
rises off a river—like that, but in darkness.

We shift apart, embrace, shift again
as needs must. You will forget me,
Beloved, I know that, and there are
no gods to supplicate. When I return
to the landscape of the story,
it's to the human figures I turn, as if
through them I might learn to refrain
from what must at root be fear.
To be in a story is a small allowance
of what feels free. To be in a story
is to study the self by forgetting it.
Meanwhile there's this daily life
gathering blow-down branches
for kindling; digging the garden,
listening to the river, to the wind,
to the owl; calling back to the owl
as we both sift what is, watching mist
reflected on the river as it lifts
into actual, open sky. I wait
for the story to continue, if it will.
What remains? There's a spray of fern
near her foot as Eurydice turns back
into a mist, as she must. Does she see it?
This bit of fern, whose prism of lit dew
as yet clarifies nothing . . .

Night Thoughts

They're on the move again, across the soundless
moonlit snow, five deer
single file along the narrow trail they deepen
night after night with their heart-shaped
hooves. Shivering, I watch them.
Back in bed, in flannel up to my nose,
I listen and listen. In my mind
already the pipes have frozen
and burst, water in a cascade
that resembles plumes of ice down rock face
along the interstate. In my mind
this house is a hovel of ice; outside
wolves howl, opposing armies
clash and scatter, a blue hand
sticks out of the snow. Almost,
I reach to take it. I'm here alone—
no, I'm not alone, I'm one of the women
left to wander crazed in snow,
the men conscripted, the villages burned.
And then here it is, like a revision of history,
the click of the furnace. O blessed click!
Of course by now I'm too awake
to sleep, and because there's something else
I don't want to remember,
and perhaps to spice the residue of my fear,
I tell myself the story of the monk
who's fallen just over the lip of a cliff.
There he is, holding on to a root
that's slowly coming loose,
and if that's not enough, a tiger
crouches above him on the precipice.
Just then, as if an invisible furnace
clicks on, he discovers within his reach
on the cliff face the single bounty
of an inauspicious planting,
a beautiful berry, fully ripe. Serenely,
the monk picks the berry and eats—delicious!

And as he falls, I realize what's at work
in this poem and all the rest I write.
Each poem I rescue my fear with a berry.
One could say it works: the fear vanishes.
So does the berry, and, momentarily, so do I.
To vanish is to live at the heart of the matter;
to vanish is to live at the lip of invitation,
embraced by emptiness and great joy.
Just so, one night after zazen-kai,
freezing cold on the beach, last birds wheeling
over the snow at the edge of the ocean,
at the edge of the world, clear how we felt,
we reached out for each other,
no hope of remedy or rescue, no time for fear.
There was only the moment, and the embracing.
Just that. When we walked back over the dunes,
I could see as if from a great height, as if
from the other side of death—two figures
ink-brushed on groundless black and white,
two figures along a curve of road as if in a painting
by Charles Chu—who, whenever he was done,
bless him, lifted his brush, stepped back
from his work, and let loose a tremendous *Ha!*

Soap

I can't breathe. If I were honest,
I'd admit to the under-my-skin damp
called loneliness, called fear.
If courageous, I'd swallow hard
and say to fear, "Come sit right down—
be fear at the head of the table."
And serve fine wine, cheese and bread,
tomatoes so dead ripe their warm
earthy scent fills the air the way
honeysuckle suckles the night.
I'd confess to the itch of expectation,
the itch of attachment; I'd display
the bruises on my arms—proof
of my struggles. As if fear, in his crisp
white shirt and black Tevas,
could be impressed by fearlessness,
perseverance, compassion, or skill.
Fear knows all about evasion.
So I confess it. I say it aloud:
I'm afraid.

        Without further word,
looking fear straight in the eye,
I begin to take off my clothes.
I know, I know, it surprises me, too.
But a stir of wind blows through
the open windows,
and I hear the tree frogs loudly
tweeting their coded messages for sex.
I begin to breathe.
Fear, purely sensed, takes a mere
ninety seconds to crest
and fall away (this is a fact)—
lingering only when one feeds it
the custard of stories and lies.
Oh, how fear then flexes his muscles!
But say we
        lean into each other,

dear fear. Let's be groundless,
curious lovers. Let's be Quakers
and clouds. Let's stay present
to the steamy pour of the shower,
to the curve of the soap on skin.
Let's melt into this feeling—fear
in my knees, in my spine. Fear
between my breasts. Fear nesting
in my armpits, fear slippery on the soles
of my feet. Dear fear, let's give
a good soaping to your cock and to my
well you get the idea. We're soaping
a doorway through uncertainty
to freedom. As we soap, behind us
vast space and light open up.
There, there, my darling. Let me
take care of you. More
sandalwood scent? A good hard
rub to the scalp? Relax. We'll rinse
and watch the suds bubble down the drain.
You can trust me. You can trust me. Just let go.

Playing Mozart at the Town Dump

The concerto in D streams out the moon roof.
Inside the car the air is ripe with Mozart,
watermelon rind, cat litter, stale beer bottles,
napkins infused with fish oil, pickle juice,
loneliness, and a mouse nest I shook free
from a flannel sheet folded away and meant
to be saved as a drop cloth. It's andante time
at the dump. High noon. On the lookout for Ralph,
who likes to ask about my absent husband
with his hand reaching for the small of my back,
I fling paper, glass, and tin into the maw of one bin
and the unsorted detritus of daily life into the other.
On the take-me table there's a wine glass,
clay pots from Mexico, commonplace plastic
toys, and a toaster. I've brought it a book
with a broken spine and a box of old LP's.
Back at the car, Mozart quickens and spills
his genius onto the talk at the nearest tailgate,
two men in sweats, leaning back, at ease
with their belly fat and old boots. Mozart
raises the tempo and gives one ball cap a flip,
but the men don't notice. Their talk is
more contemplative than you'd think.
One man tells about a friend's recent bypass
and *renewed* heart—the word's his. He says
the surgeon split him up the middle like a hog.
"It makes you think," the older one says,
and he pulls out of his hatchback a large print,
nicked and torn on its cardboard backing—
it's Renoir's luncheon party on the river.
Brightly colored parasols and tables,
the wine uncorked, the women and men florid.
Renoir—it must be noon in all his paints,
the impression of light so this-worldly
it's another world entirely, and ours. Or is it?
At the river restaurant just yesterday, the sun
blew in green gusts, dappling the white linens

on the tables, the sun afloat in the glasses
of bourgeois Chablis. Across the river
in the little park by a beer joint, two men
with loud voices: "You're a tough guy, huh?"
one yelled and slapped the other man's face,
then made to punch his ear. Then did.
Both men had ponytails and a misplaced sense
of the Sixties and its abandoned protests,
having run through too many motorcycles
and one-night stands, no place to sleep,
too much straight-no-chaser, who knows?
They socked each other in the gazebo,
drew blood, yelling *fuck* one too many times
for the wait-staff and the river customers
who couldn't intervene, but wanted to.
A few looked annoyed. Someone called the cops.
There were sirens, handcuffs, and in the quiet
after the last crunch of gravel under the tires,
a sense of smutty resolution. "Show's over,"
a waiter announced to the swordfish specials,
the tacos, lush salads, and lobster rolls.
At the dump now, where no one's wasted,
I hear the man on his way to recycle Renoir
say, "I feel for the guy." And because
he's turned his back and cleared his throat
to hide his feelings, I believe him.
"It could happen to any one of us,"
he mumbles beneath the soaring cadenzas
and inversions, now spritely, now sonorous—
Mozart, whose body was wrapped in a torn shroud
and dumped into a pauper's grave before sun-up.

Pounding the Rice

For those who know each moment is precious
an urgent patience unfolds . . .

As when Hui-Neng, a heartbeat away from the Master
he'd traveled miles and a myriad of past lives to see,

was welcomed and rebuffed at once—
sent off to the temple granary to pound the rice.

For eight years he pounded rice.
Did he use a flail? Wield a mallet? Stomp his feet, or dance?

The light would have been dusty.
Did he mutter? Sneeze? Say nothing? Weep, or laugh?

I imagine he watched each moment expand,
relaxing into his sadness, if that's what he felt,

until even the sadness was sweet,

and a bright moon
shone from the half-moons on his work-worn fingers . . .

He who couldn't read or write, who was homely and poor.

He who could see in each rice grain, abundance; in each moment,
nothing left out.

Winter Figs

Each day offers a vision. Yesterday,
a woman clothed with the sun—around her,
poppies red and radical. I was reading
The Book of Revelations, who knows why.
You remember the sky rolling up like a scroll,
the earthquake in which stars
fall like winter figs from the trees.
In a poem by Seferis, he sees
in the midst of a vision this earth
as an archaeological dig
above which the goddess rises into the sky.
The earth was becoming . . . our own,
he wrote, perhaps with a shaking hand.
And each day offers a story—each of us
has a story to tell, though we don't know
how it ends. As for me, this morning
I'm a lace maker by a window in Devon
a hundred years back, straining my eyes
as I stitch replicas of leaf and stone,
web, ripple, cattail, moon. I'm stubborn,
I'm losing my eyesight, I'm being replaced
by a machine, and still I make the world
survive me in intricate tablecloths
and shawls, the way song survives
in one who's losing her memory. No words
left for what she means or feels, yet
as words falter, or won't come, she hums
a melody, and into thin air rises
lace-lyric, the delicate shadow each thing is,
as she lifts and holds it into the failing light.

River Requiem

All day hard rain—now it's night, raw mist,
the river a surge of mud smell and omen.
In its tumult, the world of form and foment
skirls by, it builds and dissolves as clouds do,
but faster, as on the dark surface of the river
loose lariats and loops of white foam
sent downriver by the waterfall's cascade,
braiding and unbraiding, rush along—
a kind of writing hard to read, but also
as clear as the petals and ashes on the Ganges.
It's hard not to think of the afterlife—
which is to say, the next moment—
as whatever's unknown overspills and floods
what now is. And there's joy in this,
and in the heart's pounding out its mantra
god god god god god . . . Not that I live
to embrace disquiet only, but here it is.
Perhaps the opposite of peace isn't tumult,
but either one, peace or tumult, at a standstill.
Who wouldn't open wide to life's rushing
through? Each petal, each crust of ash
more precious now that I'm hearing
a deeper whisper as the river surges by,
you will die: yes, you will; you, too; you will die.

Flower

—to Marilyn

In a dream you came to me and said,

I bow to the sky, to the surge of wind

and to the clouds
shape-shifting outside the hospital window.

You said,

Long ago I bowed to the old tree
anchored in the earth by my dooryard, gnarled

and shyly leafing out.

What must it be like, the swollen belly,
the stents, the pain meds,

the needles

your mind whirling, and those moments
you return

to yourself, grateful
for those who, loving you, hold you—

but cannot take the pain away. Nor know what to pray for.

No dream, the hibiscus,
its one bud in a flourish of color, unfolds

by your river window. At night,
a shimmer of white light reflected from its source

high over the river overflows form
and name and pools on the wall inside your room.

I make a vow. Not to write an elegy for you,
who are

a world, a wholeness, an unbreakable O.

Oh, but I have been staring at my hands,
thinking about

that flower lifted up by the dying Buddha,

the flower that made one wise disciple smile—
and here you are,

each gesture, each breath,
each muscle and nerve-ending, each cell,

each tiny mitochondria

whipping its luminous tail in the cosmic swirl
you are of sun and starlight—

every waking moment,

and your wisdom, your mercy, your capacity to love—
all of it, all of it . . .

here you are, light turning into light.

The Unexpected

She's made it out of her body, out of the fire—
and now her ashes,

unmarked by all that came before, will sift through
the long-fingered Aegean.

One of us will dip her hand into the cold brine,
not yet able to understand

how to feel. Another will feel too much.

Some of the ash will ride the wind, some will
settle into a pool of silence

within a shoreline shell. *Use it for once*, Rilke
said of emptiness.

Be the shell, yet sing the lift and settle of the sea,

the echo in our blood. Be the cello just before
the unexpected

rake of the bow across the strings. Or do nothing,
lie there in the quiet morning—

somewhere, unburdened of any self-maneuver,
a tulip opens.

We are the mischief of ash even now. Any one of us,
in an instant, may be free.

A Whisper

Draw close. Everyone you love, and everyone you don't,
will someday die—you know this.
Resist or embrace it, either way sadness as pungent
as jasmine sooner or later fills you. Let it settle,
let all your holy striving settle.

There's a covert in your body where either *yes* or *no*
is the answer—and it doesn't matter which you say.
Be there long enough, every morning
sun streams through the original window.

Evolution

This tall fern has a midrib so sturdy
I can pluck its broad width of green
and wave it before my face as I walk
the lane, the gnats and the deerflies
shooed pell-mell as the air ripples away
from my body. I'm no longer a target.
Do this enough, in three million years
I'll have evolved a frontal "tail"
to cool my passion. Should the heat
and human nature continue for eons,
ferns may be as lofty as oaks,
we humans a scurry of ants—fancy ants
with rudimentary green tails in our heads,
still addicted to sweets, to nasturtiums,
to love, and to the crooked
avenues of desire that bring it home
to our little colonies in the fern groves . . .
Well, so much for this morning's
vow to let fantasy fall away. No more,
I said, this substitute life that remains
stuck in my head. Too bad—I perform
so beautifully on that stage. Whatever
the right words, I say them. I'm exciting.
You're bound by my spell: you even
love me—yes, you over there,
turning your head my way. But that
lowdown queasiness, the tight inner frown—
how seldom, if ever, I acknowledge these.
When I do, and if I listen faithfully,
what I hear is childhood's bat cave echo,
You'll never be good enough.
That's what I believe, apparently.
Not evolution. Not the slow work of God.
Today, Rumi writes, *a new madness is
trying to set us free.* If so, says my head,
you can exchange old madness for new.
My head calls me *you*—and who is that?

I ask again and again, until at last
my slow-going stalactite consciousness
adds a glow-in-the-dark inch of joy—
then opens as daylilies do into a wide sky's
uplift of light and air. To end a poem
in a mix of metaphors may be madness,
but I've just learned—waving my fern
down the lane, following what isn't
and what is, wherever they lead me—the real
work is not the poem, but what moves me to it,
evolving into this good silence. I won't claim more.

What It Takes

The fire won't light—no kindling—
so I twist and ball the daily news, then add
the darker moments of my childhood,
hair from my hairbrush,
hollow laughter, and then like wisps of lint
from the trap of the clothes dryer,
whatever remains in me of aspiration,
expectation, longing.
It takes a while to penetrate
the great truth of fire's benevolent
destruction, what it
teaches as the logs at last ignite
and a riff of radiance surrounds
each dense and materially
worthy or unworthy
thought of mine that clutters
the infinite space of the heart—the heart,
which only wants to open.
My god, what it takes to ignite the dross
of cherished illusions—then
stay put and watch the burning.
The sound is of wind over the vast star fields.
Forgiveness may be like this. Also, grace.

Passage

And then a bird flew into my body and nested in the cuff of my shoulder.
This is the mystery of pain—it can sing.

I hear the wind differently now. I breathe, and my ribs are the cirrus of clouds.
There's a river in my wrist. Daily I practice

eclipse, although ordinary loss will do. At night I ripen beneath a hush of stars.

Without Thinking about It

Even though

I tie bells onto the lower branches of the cedar
five bells
smallish, brass . . .

the liturgy of everyday life
goes on, without

disruption or explanation
silently

even in rain or brusque wind . . .

All day the heart—which has
no clapper—
makes itself heard

moving inside the bone cage

softly,
as over moss, footfall by footfall

I am drawn deeper into what may be
the certainty that

not knowing if faith or doubt keeps me here . . .

keeps me, here.

Old Cloth

I would like to describe the heart
as a first-century ode describes it—
split open, sending up flowers and fruits.
Heart is a seed pit that breaks open
in two directions, the root taking hold
in the earth, the stalk shooting off
into a field of milky stars,
which right now I can sense beneath
my pillow.   I'd like to describe the heart
as Solomon did, but here I am,
in the dream holding a newborn
who's been split in two just below
the navel. I rush away from
the birthing room—the child is divided
but still lives, and I cradle her.
Thank you, I cry. *I'm sorry. Forgive me.*
And the dreaming mind
shifts to a deeply cut grave, the child
at the bottom of the dark pit
waving her little arms
as someone I call an oaf starts to shovel
dirt right onto the child—
the oaf doesn't know what he's doing.
Why doesn't he pay attention?
The angel does.
                    Here she is, intimate
with spirit, fed by its insights. I try
to follow her breath as she breathes
in and out with the child. *Look,* she says,
I have also made your bed with sheets
as gold as the iris by the gate of the Infinite.
Fresh sheets and an old cloth from India—
anything torn has been patched
and stitched seamlessly together.
Now she gives me the also-mended
child.

How I love her small feet,
her knees, her thighs, her genitals.
I love her belly and nipple buds and lungs.
I love her arms and her hands, her eyes
and her ears, her mouth, and her mind.
Most of all I love her heart, which sings
like a struck bowl. The bowl is her cradle.
I am her cradle, her riverbed and orchard
and nest.
            I would like to describe the heart
without words. I would like the dream
to open into a great light in which I am
neither cradle nor dark pit, neither angel
nor oaf nor child—but I'm standing now
at the border where one world dims
and another brightens; where what is called
waking up is the flowering of innate intention;
where, whether in garden solitude
or on the crowded streets of commerce,
inner and outer, when they meet, stand close,
their eyes open, and their mouths, touching tongues.

Door

Morning sunlight, glass door,
dust—an even
film of it on the steep glass
which also
reflects and fills as does the eye
with forsythia and the subtle
greening just beginning
in the bare trees out there.
Out there. In here.
I want to believe that what is
is not separate—and yet
the illusion of boundaries
is solid. I knock on it, bring
a soft cloth, soap and water.
Now a bend in the backbone,
an arc of reach, gentle
pressure, polishing . . .
In a poem I wrote years back
the glass I wiped clean
and polished turned into
your body, Beloved,
into love cry and migrating birds
come home, on fire.
Now it is the dust on things,
and of things,
that calls, that woos, that whispers,
We are made to be seen through.
Yes. And we are made to shatter.
Made to smell the rain-rinsed air
rushing the door I am no other than
threshold, breath . . .

Riverkeeper

Wanting to be that place where inner
and outer meet, this morning
I'm listening to the river inside—
also to the river out the window, river
of sun and branch shadow, muskrat
and mallard, heron, and the rattled cry
of the kingfisher. Out there is a tree
whose roots the river has washed so often
the tree stretches beyond itself, its spirit
like mine, leaning out over the water, held
only by the poised astonishment
of being here. This morning, listening
to the river inside, I'm sinking into a stillness
where what can't be said stirs beneath
currents of image and memory, below strata
of muons and quarks, now rushes, now hushes
and pools, now casts a net of bright light
so loosely woven there's a constellation
afloat on the surface of the river, so still
I can almost hear it weave in and out—
interstellar, intercellular—and isn't it
truly all one, one world, no *in* or *out*, no *here*
or *there*, seamless, as a lily about to open
from just here into everywhere, is. Just is.
Restful lily. Lucky lily. To bloom must feel
like a river's brightening at daybreak,
or a slow kiss, a throb in the elapse of time,
a shudder of heron shadow flying over
shallows that are merely the apparent
skim of a depth whose bottomless surface
seeps everywhere, bloom and retraction,
an anchored flow that upholds city
and cathedral, bridge and gate,
Orion, odd toad in the Amazon, blue dragonfly,
what it is to love . . . Spoil a river, you spoil all this.

How Long the Long Winter

Awake in the middle of the night, the river
cracks with language, the ice of it
a heave of squares and oblongs.
Only the waterfall, its cold spray
frosting nearby juts of stone with lace,
continues to tumble as if it will
never cease to move and be. Once it was,
we lay down together, two lakes
touching. "I want to do to you
what spring does to the lilac," I whispered.
Not an idle fancy, or vain—I'm drawn
to what any one moment might make
of its impermanence. That's all we have.
We know the body dies. We say the spirit
doesn't . . . but, I don't know.
In five billion years the sun will take out
the earth and all life, if there's still
life left. Billions more, and the expanding
universe will reach its limit and recede,
raveling back into the nothing
from which nothing comes.
It will be as if we were never here.
Love, joy, the music our bodies make—once
we've vanished, what happens to these,
these streaks of light released
from within us to blow about like pollen
among the blossoming stars? What happens to
spirit when the material universe
of star birth and sun's warmth is no more?
How long the long silence in which it lies
dormant? How long the long winter of no
river, no meander, no waterfall rainbow
or ocean splendor—before the random
spark ignites and out of what seems impossible
love, once again, comes love?

Passage

Strike a bell or a singing bowl,
you hear a vibrant ringing, then the ringing through, that afterthought

of sound at rest in silence as it floats off in search of the boundless.

Ring the bowl of your body,
you cry out and sink into the river that sings

in your sleep and beneath your thoughts on waking—

making love is part of the practice of listening. Say *yes* quickly, or say *no;*
say nothing at all. You know this is true.

You have always known, even when you didn't,

what sings you into being, what releases,
what continues without you, ringing through.

Continuing the Story

You are not here, Beloved, but I know
you remember how mist
rises off a river, and the story
continues, as it must,
Eurydice just past the threshold
but not yet embraced
by the darker recesses of the cave.
If there is light, it is dusk light.
She is still apparent,
watching as the lifeline in her hand
turns to dry streambed,
her breath to a light wind in the reeds.
And Orpheus? He's a confluence
of birdcall in the meadow.
Bless loss, Eurydice whispers. She can
still form words, although soon
they will lift in a cloud of clatter, like birds
in the pine grove. And her
mind? Her mind is a mirror
from which the world now recedes,
as once it had advanced, confirming her—
broken cloud, empty gate,
the throat of a flower, the thick
bright beak of a thrush; olive trees
on the sloping hill, each callus
of lichen on stone, the shiver of a leaf.
Heartbeat, yes. Footfall, yes.
And then his face . . . She can still
see the face of her lost beloved.
After love, she used to hold his head
against her breasts as he slept, and once,
their bodies slippery as fish,
they made love in the river.
River is lure and longing; river is
the deepest bow one can make
to the fact of being wed to a cosmos
light years deep. *Bless loss,*

she says to the fern by her foot.
And while I do not understand, not really,
the story ravels into actual rain,
and the grass, the stones, the cedars,
the pond—everything I daily conjure,
blurs. What was I thinking of, all those years
trying to be good, trying to be known,
trying not to falter into loneliness?
Nearer death, I bow. Here I am.
Once, I don't know why, water formed
in the hollows of the planet's surface,
primeval pools so still they held
the furthest furnace flares of the stars.
And in those pools the cosmos
turned toward itself, aware of itself
for the first time. As deep as all space
and light, as deep as the visible,
I am even now a ripple in that pool, Beloved—
and this, it occurs to me now, is freedom.

The Door

Neither inside nor outside
there's a door.

Do you hear it rattling in the wind?

Beyond measure, this wind—
still you sit there
and don't ask

What is it?
Not even, *What's on the other side?*

And now the rain arrives. At any time
you might have
unlatched

yourself, shouting *Here I am,*
and been

lifted into the gold light that rinses
each cell.

It rains harder. Never mind—
you might still

come stand here in the downpour,
raise up your arms—

maybe a little higher, that's it—

throw back your head
and let the rain
fall through you, until *you're*

the door flown open in the wind.

When you're not your body,
you don't get wet.

Opening and Closing the Book of Changes

Before completion, some days I throw coins or yarrow sticks to ask the oracle,
How do I find God?

Or I speak of the soul as if it were the unison call of the red-crowned crane.

A voice whispers, *the cure for the pain is in the pain . . .*
that inside my tiredness,
                there's a well.

I'd ask the awakened, *How did you do it?* But mum's the word.

Here's what I think:
                this one opens like a temple gate;
that one, at the moment morning light begins.

Another may require the surgeon's knife.

You can live by proxy; you can dream.
You can feed the fire geranium petals to make the flames more red.

Meanwhile,
                the old fox of legend moves over the ice, alert to its cracking,
alert to the rushing river beneath.

From floe to floe she leaps, she lifts her tawny tail and does not get it wet—
steely haunches, dainty padded feet.

Clouds and Moon

Today there are clouds and deep puddles
the color of coffee in the dirt road.
For breakfast, an orange. Toast, with
butter and Gillian's homemade marmalade.
I practice sounding English like her,
I don't know why. Daffodil's are up,
I wander lonely as a cloud. I remember
a friend and his melancholy. Wonder
if it's catching. Wonder, if I feel it
fully, will I find the gift sadness cloaks?
I brush my hair; I brush it again, try
a different barrette to hold it. Forget that—
I shake out my hair. *Who can stay still?*
Which is the way to Mount Wutai?
I go outside with the dead English poets
and the crazy cloud Chinese, and I walk.
In the night the brook has washed over
the road in a great slur of mud and leaves.
I admire the fact of natural forces. I admire
each one of the sodden sticks I yank
from the leafy roil left behind in the road.
The more sturdy ones I fling into the brook
to see how fast they flush with the torrent.
Most I place to the side of the road
in a bundle so tidy it resembles kindling
someone will return for. I study
my empty hands. By now, it's afternoon,
how did that happen? Here it is,
my whole life a continuous upwelling
I can't catch or hold. The bottom
falls out of the bucket, the moon flows through.

Passage

I watch my hands turn into clouds. Now I give back to the river
his touch, his body, the field of stars,
the buds that opened in the lace of early spring snow.

I take the river inside and moving like the river learn how
river has a rhythm all its own through spring rain, summer
drought, tidal ebb and flow or flood,

a new river each moment. Ask Heraclitus.

Ask, When am I most happy? And the river whispers, *Now.* And when
least happy? *Now.* When am I in love? *Now.* And not in love?
Constantly inconstant, coursing or mirror still,

let river fill that *something missing* in my heart. Let it rest in me,
and I in it. Let it take me where it will. Where before, I couldn't,
or wouldn't, go. From which, even now, I draw back.

Sunday Morning

Fragrance of honeysuckle in the pool of a green jar . . .

Last night's rain has settled into beads along the soffit
and brightened the facets of the window screen.

I'm listening for after-sound, wind-stir . . .

Slowly last night's rain
is drawn into the root hairs of everything out there.

It travels unheard, unasked.

At times the holy is a bell that flares and flings out its call notes.

Or as now, a bell rope, slack,
that wills not to steeple silence but to plumb it.

There is nothing to pray to, yet everything is prayer.

Near the Ocean

Old prayer rugs, books, a jar of blue iris.
By the window an empty celadon bowl
to hold the light, when there is light—
in the dream I bow to what is intimate
and near, and only gradually do I see
beyond the morning's open door
a sweep of ocean, blue and gray and white.
There's a tall pole jammed into the sand,
on top of it a stack of folded clothing.
The mind—which wants to know what's up
and is passing itself off as inquiry—asks,
Are you in the world, or is the world in you?
I only know I'm dreaming. And look,
on the indoor panel of the dark wood door
there's an elegant effigy, which I recognize
as my likeness, carved in high relief,
then oiled and polished. But I'm not that,
I whisper. *Before Abraham was, I am*—
it's the shift in tense unbolts the way
to the formless, the unborn, the holy.
God, if you will. God, even if you won't.
And so I stand in the dream, which is to say,
right here, stunned and silent. Waves are coming in.
In a whir of wings, the sun lifts into view.
Just the sun, as it is. Wind in my hair.
Salt on the bare skin of my body. If I lift
my pen from paper now, what happens?
No one says a word. No one is here. Let's find out . . .

Footprints

Years living here, I have become
just this morning's
white sky. Years, and yet
there must remain a jot of soil
or grass that has not
felt my weight.
It's the nature of walking
that one leaves between each footfall
a gap—
as the watercolorist's brush
may skip in its stroke over paper,
opening a window in the blue.
A *holiday*, it's called.
No going back, no filling in.
Each day letting go of desire,
wanting
more and more to live in that ellipsis . . .

Passage

Into steep blue distance the blue heron flies, into the vanishing point.
The river surges, taking me with it.

And when it is dark enough within, I am whatever is presently
ready to take form but hasn't, yet.

Readiness itself is a form of patience that neither wonders
nor expects, nor is disciplined . . . unless stillness is a discipline.

And it's essential to believe in nothing, to feel its presence,
its loving-kindness and vast aloneness, its love cry, its weight.

One tremor, then another. All of it *withindoors* . . . shimmering.

The Cry

No longer any wish to give a name
to the one vine
that unfurls its many blooms
continually beside the door,
and whose tendrils
brush lightly at my sleeves,
coming and going. Sorrow daily
changes to wonder, and a cry—
windswept, and yet
as particular as the click of a stone
footfall dislodges—
moves throughout space and time.
No hinge or heart-latch to it.
Unsought, it comes to you.
Unbinds and scours.
A residue of all that has been stored
as if in large clay jars
in the inner sanctum of a tomb. And it is
entirely and only what you are. A cry.

After Innocence

Within the plum tree's froth and bloom,
imagination steered me,
rapt, into the star fields, and I hummed—
hymns, most likely. Now I break down
in a mutter of tears for no reason—yes,
I should calm down. As a child,
I was the plum tree's rough bark
and fuzzy scent; the night sky was vast
and near, the stars a somatic dazzle.
Oh, that was long ago! I was unified
and clear. Since then I've either
looked away or held on too tight,
unwilling to see what I've cherished
become a lovely clutter in the heart.
But tonight I hear you, No one—
Let the petals fall—
and into the ringing stillness,
where I may wait forever for all I know,
I let them go. What's in doubt for once,
No one, *isn't* you. You exist, if only
as an odd willingness to let my spirit
be empty of everything I thought
I felt or heard or saw or had to have
if happiness were to continue.
I have nothing now. The nothing's you.

Not to Remain Altogether Silent

All the time I kept you out of my poems,
you found a way into my body instead.
Instead of your becoming another word
for dove or wrist bone, owl or stone,
you've become the impulse that has me
raise cairns to mark my way. You're
what all verbs traverse, a fuse for the urge
to look at what I can't see within what I can;
also the stillness inside me as wind-riven
leaves are driven over the roof shingles
into the night. Kindled by earth and sky,
you're the touch of a tongue on my skin,
contingent and mortal; and the shy,
reluctant love of faithfulness to what I feel
when at times I think *there are no gods*.
You are in me what is crucial and crucible
when the soul, in its root-fire, lasers and welds
each fissure and craze line of my loving elusive,
if pervasive, you. How stark it is to be alive—
and, although absence is the form you take
in what we call the world, how durable . . .

Rude Drift

What if now I say *you*—and intend that
to frame a space the holy
might inhabit? I saw such a space once,
in early morning calm—stalks
that had been pushed into the lake bed,
bent and linked to make a hemisphere
which, completed by its own reflection
in the water, became a sphere.
I don't know if the artist believed in
anything more than his own clarity,
but there for anyone to see
he devised an empty self-reflective
Whole—a way to posit . . . *you*—
your emptiness
completing our contingency.
So is this the famous Incarnation?
Now you moor in the moment, then
ripple off. Now you rhyme, if slant,
then don't. You complete me,
only to let me drift stalk by stalk away.
Why hast thou forsaken me? Only
someone really intimate asks
that question. I don't know
whether to whisper this or raise my voice.
You should be with me as I suffer.

Ripe

In the local moment hear the rasp
of the dog's tongue on his fur
and on his cushion while music ferrets
its way through the interstices
of the trees between this house
and Amos Lake, where the party
is nearly over. Midnight.
Thinking spoils everything, don't you
think? Tonight I choose to be
guided by . . . you give it a name,
No one, I can't. That's why
I'm talking to you, practicing
your presence, as did Brother Lawrence.
Doubtless he'd wiggle his toes, listen
to the mosquito whine, mistake
the engine noise of the cargo jet
for distant thunder, then tell you
about it. No prayers by rote.
I'd be drawn so close to the Source,
there's no distance between self
and other—isn't this how to live?
And this is not an easy thought.
The upsurge of violence in Missouri,
Palestine, India, Ukraine
boards any piety like a pirate,
making off with my peace of mind.
Now I'm a refugee. Now an owl,
now a cooling current of air
from the open window.
By the moon's light I can see
the residue of milk and cinnamon
smudged along the glass of the cup
I drank down to help me sleep.
Now I'm a cup—empty but for a mission
I have no name for. I long to let go.

I long for you to take me over. I long
to sink my teeth into you, no longer
a ripe idea but a peach
about to turn if I don't eat it, and right now.

Two Trees

I want to know *you* the way I know
summer's ending—the light
low enough late afternoons to shadow
the clapboards; an undercoat of burnt
sienna singeing the leaves of a maple;
"tobacco juice" on the hand that traps
and tries to hold any grasshopper;
over here, two trees blighted nearly
to their summits. The die-off's started,
a kind of seasonal dementia.
Sometimes the beautiful are also good,
an old woman said to me, after I'd done
a small kindness anyone could do.
My Beloved's hands are bruised
where the aides have to hold him—
it's harder for him, incontinent,
to feel any gratitude for help.
None of us really wants to *need* help.
As late light brightens the bones
of the birch, whose limbs shine
like the raised arms of Krishna's beloved
dancing in a glade, I become aware,
No one, how relieved I am you don't
step right up and clarify the mystery.
With you it's all sparks of light,
tints and hints, perhaps an occasional
bolt out of the blue to shake loose
a sense of terror that may evolve
somehow into clarity,
emergent even in decline and ruin.
I look about and find whatever I see
unfinished. Forget heaven. Refuse it,
in fact. I love what's wretched and redolent
and raw about you—*in* me,
through me, *as* me. And yet, as we both
know, the love I express
is too easy. Something in me must die.

Motive for Praise, Perhaps

I have friends who, talking about death,
claim it's not death but dying
they fear—the process, the pain,
the lack of privacy, the pain. They're too
savvy to turn to you, No one,
as a personal comforter. "It's not about me,"
one says. Another speaks of
the injustice of self-pity. As for me,
I think, with practice,
fear becomes a koan that ramifies,
then wrings the mind
into the stand-still clarity of *non-thinking*—
where you live, No one.
"Things fall apart, the *memoir* cannot hold,"
my husband, on the cusp
of memory loss, scrawled in the margin—
story our centre, he believed. Tell me
about pain, how subtle it is. How sly.
And tell I do. I tell and tell, until
the telling numbs like denial
or suddenly surges, rousing its own
version of an afterlife. No one, your story,
if you have one, is the birth of stars—
so terrifying and vast
the mind implodes, collapsing every
metaphor I've heard or read or said.
Your story, it's selfless. If love,
it's love that continues without us.
And . . . so quiet.

The Full Catastrophe

Why is it, No one, this morning,
your provisional no-name
fails to delight me? Your presence
bears down on me
as if promising a specific oblivion.
Worse, I'm afraid I'll look inside
and find I'm the same
woman I ever was—if a river,
one that swings like a hammock
or an elegy. Or that
merely floating toward you,
not sinking into, I'll be
washed into the shallows of a lesser desire.
There's always desire. Who
wants to admit to the full catastrophe?
I wait a moment, and who appears
but Heraclitus, in the guise of
Anthony Quinn, Zorba dancing,
his arm around his friend's shoulder,
both of them stepping lightly
at the edge of the sea
all rivers come to. Footnote *sea*
as a metaphor for the formless
essential majesty of Being aware of itself
as Being—but alas, this morning
a storm at sea washes me
into that drifting continent of refuse
held in place somewhere out in the Pacific
by tides and swirling currents—
and I see it, as if from the air,
as a mandala of my condition.
Here I am, adrift in the fact of flow,
unaware of what I'm avoiding—
then suddenly
I'm arrested by the cold severity
in my Beloved's eyes. "I hate this," he says.
"Perhaps he will kill himself."

He may speak of himself
in the third person, but he's not fooled by
the illusory nature of hope or the self,
nor will he accept consolation.
"Things have a way of turning out
well in the end," I once offered,
and he said, "That's not true."
He knows I love him. And he knows
he's not home as home was. Now
his home is loss; mine's a river.
I can bear my own pain. Just not his.
When he was a young man, he feasted
on lamb and ouzo. The lord
of the taverna had three daughters,
and they entered the room of laughter
and bouzouki "shyly turning their
wrists," he wrote, "toward the ceiling
as though reaching high for grapes."
Did anyone at that moment sense
the great stare of oblivion bearing down?
Heraclitus was at the table nearest a river
no one could hear because of the music.
No one, where were you?

Richer than Prayer or Vow

As the sun sinks behind a rim of trees,
darkness rises from down low
in the grass and scattered leaves.
The wind also rises, breathing on
embers that flare into stars. Tonight
at last I release a residue of weariness
I could mistake for worthlessness—
yes, I am kneeling on bare earth,
something like forgiveness
rising from the damp ground
and root of humility. It's worth
saying: I've done harm,
I've broken my vow—more than one,
more than once. But if I am only
the sum of my ignorance and error,
then the dark is dark indeed,
so unlike what opens in me
when I say, No one, your name,
richer than prayer or vow.
Remember who you are.
That whisper I heard once on waking—
No one, was it you?
No answer, but the wind lifts, and I listen,
wanting only to be still enough
to sense what may once again
kindle and rush along the riverbed
of my spine, sweeping before it
whatever in me is tormented
or broken. I have no words for
what I may become.
Words are only a way to breathe
as I struggle to stand, then stand—
nowhere more holy than this ground.

Middle Distance, Morning

One by one, leaves spindle in the wind,
the clock runs down, the cricket's
chirr continues. Each year I try
to catch the moment the chirring ceases
and silence takes on its winter timbre.
Each year I miss. Doing nothing,
poised for a flash from the Absolute,
awaiting rest from unrest,
I'm blessed by uncertainty,
steadied more by loss than by the snare
of an embellished self-possession.
And no, I'm not lonely, No one, not
in the midst of *all my relations*,
as an old woman called the living world
around her, from quark to cairn,
from stone to a flash of wings
in the updraft. The grass is wet, and mist
rises wherever the sunlight falls.
The maple rising from its bright ground
in middle distance
is a shapely fluidity that anchors
a shining web to woodbine and one
branch of a yearling crabapple.
Perhaps imagination's only a fling
of slim thread, so that Mind can walk
its own tightrope, also the heart—
in Chinese the word for mind
and the word for heart is the same.
Just now, the light shifts, and the web is
no longer visible from where I sit.
Across the pond the woods are
a darkness, a depth, a distance
beyond the edge of knowing, I write.
But there's no edge
unless I make one. In middle distance,
a red leaf finds a way
to spin in its own orbit. Now, a gold.

Praise

Anything I praise praises your secret name—
the steam of the singing kettle,
a black night with stars sparking the bright branches,
fire furling about the oak in the grate,
the savor of soup, the mango seed I suck
not to waste the sweet fruit.
Don't tell me your secret name,
No one—I want to sense it as the blind
tell words by touch, as the wind shivers
when the falcon soars from the thicket by the river,
rising with wings on fire toward the sun.

Isolable

At my age, I should be in love
with the formless—
not with the leaf I chanced on, arrested in
midair, suspended on apparently
nothing but a defiance of gravity
and law; no, not
with the leaf, nor with the (for a long time)
invisible filament that held it
at rest in emptiness.
I looked and looked and never did detect
from what the shimmering
depended—I saw nothing overhead—
and I walked on alone,
knowing no more, No one, than I had
setting out. I hadn't been praying,
but I had been searching for another
way into my life. Nor was anything settled
as I walked on. Only something better left
unspoken, understood.

Open Window

Come to the window, I hear. *It's your river, too.*
There's no one close beside me, no breath
in my ear, only cold air and late sun
aflame in the winter trees, all of it carried
by the stillness of the bright water.
As if they were husks of possessive pronouns,
mind and body fall away, and I am
the whole sky of birds
pouring now as if through a funnel
into oncoming night—such an inrush
of wings and outcry that in a flash
I understand *incarnate*.
Everything shines.
I absorb the shining, and find it again,
No one, in you, more intimate than any
lover who gives to his beloved
the taste of her body, giving it back
to her mouth by his tongue. God,
I love my life—each flash of radiance,
each ghost of grief. Why wait
for the sky to open in a waterfall of spirits
ascending and descending?
Let everything be as it is. Let everything be as it is.

Unconditional

As *the slow work of God* continues
breath by breath, the soul sinks
into a depth of leisure that allows
living as the river lives. Now
I no longer persist in telling stories
I know aren't true, however
they might comfort or thrill.
Oh, I have stories! But the protagonist,
whether flawed or idealized,
is a fiction dressed up in oak leaves,
impulse, metaphor, and the sweet
sweet myths of metamorphosis.
These days I'd rather sit by a river
and listen. Tell me, No one,
what will happen to the fields I love,
the woods, the birds that vanish
and return. Animals, friends, family—
where do they go, lives that,
quick or slow, move into a further
intensity of vibration,
then disappear? And I want to know
what happens to the heart. Not,
Can this marriage be saved? Not even
Can it be understood? Remember
the good old days of conditioned
love? Remember, "I'll do this,
if you'll do that?" Back then
the marriage had papers beside the door,
and it had to pee on them
before it learned to ask to be let out
into the endless, unconditional
bounty of the wind, the trees, the stars.
No longer. I love my Beloved
no matter what, no matter how
or why. It's as if the river has deepened
its channel and widened out.
The feeling remains, Teresa of Ávila

mused, *that God is on the journey, too.*
How does it happen? Some days,
I only am that I am
when known by what I do not know.
And that mystery, No one? You.

Passage

Once in sunlight I pinned to a clothesline a cotton sheet, a plane of light
sheer as the mind of God,

before we imagined that mind creased by a single word.
With my hand I smoothed any rivel, any shirr, any suggestion of pleat or furrow.

Whatever it was I wanted from that moment, I can't say. It failed to edify.
Nor did I bow.

And yet the memory holds, and there is a joy that recurs in me much as the scent
of summer abides in air dried sheets I unfold long after,

lying down in them as one might in a meadow,
as one might with a lover, as one might court the Infinite, however long it takes.

CPSIA information can be obtained
at www.ICGtesting.com
Printed in the USA
LVHW092259170919
631432LV00002B/219/P